JANE YEH was born in America in 1971 and educated at Harvard University. She holds master's degrees from the Iowa Writers' Workshop and Manchester Metropolitan University. Her chapbook, *Teen Spies*, was published in 2003 by Metre Editions. She is the recipient of a New York Foundation for the Arts Fellowship and an Academy of American Poets Prize. Currently Writer in Residence at Kingston University, she contributes articles on books and sport to *The Times Literary Supplement*, *Poetry Review*, *The Village Voice*, and *Time Out New York*. She lives in London.

JANE YEH

Marabou

CARCANET

Acknowledgements

Grateful thanks to the editors of the publications in which some of these poems first appeared: *Antioch Review*; *Boston Review*; *Grolier Poetry Prize Annual*; *LIT*; *Metre*; *New Poetries III* (Carcanet, 2002); *New Voices: University and College Prizes, 1989-1998* (The Academy of American Poets, 2002); *PN Review*; *Poems, Poets, Poetry: An Introduction and Anthology* (Bedford/St Martin's, 2002); *Poetry* (Chicago); *Poetry Review*; *Quarterly West*; *The Times Literary Supplement*; *TriQuarterly*.

The author gratefully acknowledges the support of the New York Foundation for the Arts and its grant of an Artist Fellowship.

First published in Great Britain in 2005 by
Carcanet Press Limited
Alliance House
Cross Street
Manchester M2 7AQ

A CIP catalogue record for this book is available from the British Library
ISBN 1 85754 788 8

The publisher acknowledges financial assistance from Arts Council England

Typeset by XL Publishing Services, Tiverton
Printed and bound in England by SRP Ltd, Exeter

Contents

I

II

III

I

Correspondence

I've gotten nothing for weeks. You might think of me

As dated in a blue housecoat, buttoning and unbuttoning,
Waiting you out: I have my ways

Of keeping time. When your letter comes, dogs will bark
Up and down the street. The tomatoes in the garden

Will explode like fireworks. Each day the mailman passes
In a reverie, illiterate, another cobweb

Grows across the door. Picture me
Going bald one hair at a time, combing and curling, burning

My hand on the iron once every hour: I like to
Keep myself busy. When I hear from you, *aurora*

Borealis will sweep across the sky. Every lottery ticket in my drawer
Will win. Even the mailman will know the letters

Of your name. If you bothered to notice, you would see me
Turning to gold rather slowly, bone

By bone, the way teeth come
Loose from the gums, the way animals go

Extinct, in geological time.

Double Wedding, 1615

Anne of Austria, sister of Philip IV, to King Louis XIII of France;
Isabella of Bourbon, sister of Louis XIII, to King Philip IV of Spain

We are laced taut
As an archer's bow strung with catgut, a lean

And deadly spring to the touch. At each breath
Our stomachs press whalebone, seven bent fingers

Stiff as our own ribs and wrapped in linen, leaving
The fine print of their weave on our skin. We are wired

For great things and small movements, hooped
To glide like gigantic orchids, full-

Blown, slow-footed, and deliberate
In error. Afterwards we will bear the strange marks

Of another house, gold arms on a gold collar,
But for now *no other jewels hang about our necks*

Than these: pearls knotted with string, clasped
With velvet, and fitted just the length

To choke us. This day will slip from us
Shedding marquisette, point d'esprit, zibelline, trailing

Taffeta and broché behind it; it will leave us bare-
Handed and desperate to remember what we were

Before it, and it will take everything we have
To recollect what we wore when we walked

The length of the nave without stopping, how we kept
Our eyes straight and unturning until it was over.

The Pre-Raphælites

'What *do* you mean by beauty?' In the Grosvenor Gallery
In our 'mediæval' dresses, in our rapt and utterly

Fashionable gazes, we cannot touch
The isinglass wall of these

Damned unprofitable lives. What it is
That wrecks us—
                              I was lying
In the garden, up against the barrier

The mandragora were twined like thin fingers.
Sometimes I pose when no-one is there.

Please God I am a creature of habit and well-fed. A puzzle
Like a door in a hedge that is made of hedge, inscrutable.

What it is that is wrong in me—
                              When one glove in a pair is turned inside-out
It becomes the same as the other one, but with the seams exposed.

Nobody wants to see that.
Here is a conjuror's trick:

I the disappearing girl. Look again and I turn up back in the box,
Same as before. I have not got anywhere.

Why am I, why am I caught
In the hinge of this world and it presses me, where was the wrong turn

Taken took me to the middle of the maze and gave
Me this head, these hands, this beast's face?

Adultery

I could beg but I don't have to. What it is
I couldn't say. A chronic incidence

Of cringing from the light in elevators,
Night trains, doorwells: if this heart, it clatters

Into the bin like a handful of change, if this tatty
Muzzle, it fits the crime, if strapless

Were to 'having it' as bang-up is to 'done that',
Would my position be worth a flutter?

Darkness, debt, a peep, the thrill: possession
Is theft from, proof is knowing where, love

Is blind they say, but I'm having none of it.
I've an eye to the main chance.

I look better in the dark.
Even if the phone rings now I won't stop.

Convent at Haarlem

In the seventeenth century the whitest linen in Europe was produced at Haarlem. Strips of fabric were laid out in the fields to undergo bleaching and drying.

We go out
Sprinkling bone-ash from long-handled shovels, it is dusk and the seventh

Month of repetitions. Ours is the lengthwise passage
Between March and November; we filter through the dunes

Like rainwater, keeping straight by the linen. In the brownest
Stretch of grass you could come upon me,

Above all scurrying animals and fringed about with water:
Sieved out from a sea off the Low Countries'

Polderlands, slipping the estuaries.
You would judge me a narrow sort of reclamation.

We turn in to our several labours, the spreading of rushes, the winding up
The well. In a house of silent women

You are the rotten timber, the sand that rustles under-
Foot, the crooked tallow candle's socket: yours is the slow

And graduated wearing. Once, I was the one running
Across the green lines of your fields, crossing

The blond-wood boards of the floor of your room, an original
Bit of nonsense, your doll.

Cumbria

It seems unfair to the sheep.
Now that the cull's on, they haven't a chance.
They can't help being round, contagious, and woolly.
Ghostly herds bobble slowly down the track.

Their haunting is not sinister; it is not by design.
We got left behind. Something went wrong.
An atom's half-life is the time it takes for half the mass to decay.
The half-life of a sheep is unnatural— survival of the faintest

Impression of a beast, marginalia—
Then erased. It is meaningless,
Our existing, like a note on the leg of a pigeon left blank:
No message. We can't eat

But we pretend to: that's inertia.
Like a wind-up toy, you can't unwind it.
The bolt in the head, the head on the pyre.
Then we wake up but we're not alive.

You can't take our picture. (We don't reflect light.)
What can't be observed can't be changed by the viewer.
We're listening to the wind making shapes in the sky
Like sheep, like smoke. Here we are, listening.

The Only Confirmed Cast Member Is Ook the Owl, Who Has Been Tapped To Play the Snowy White Owl Who Delivers Mail for Harry

quoted from a New York Post *article on preproduction for the first Harry Potter film*

Claw up. Claw down. Cut.
My fine eyes. My fine eyes are— Cut.

I was fluffed and plucked, like a beauty-pageant winner,
Between takes. Like a news presenter.
Could I be a news presenter?

Rider: 5 rashers bacon. 8-oz. tin mixed nuts.
2 lbs. rabbit fillets. Assorted drupes.

Between takes, I did leg-lifts in my trailer.

If asked what is your most treasured possession, I would say
The woolly toy Tracey, my personal trainer, gave me when young.
I learnt to spy it from afar, then swoop down and seize,
But only on cue. Mr Sheep goes everywhere with me now.

If I could wake up having gained one ability,
It would be the capacity for more facial expression.
It is so tedious to have one's beak set in a permanent frown.

My greatest talent is impersonation—
To simulate a person's idea of an owl.
Sadly, I owe my success to typecasting.

My greatest fear is to be found wanting.

At the premiere party, the women were not very clothed.
It is of advantage to be clad always in feathers.

I allowed fake friends to pet me.
My picture was taken several times with the boy.
I enjoy parties because otherwise I see only Tracey.
Afterwards, you wonder what the glitter was for.

II

Bad Quarto

With my low production values I'm a little

Unfinished, a tinful of rushes, cobbled together
On two rows of nails with a razor blade and ruler. I'm shot

Full of holes and jump cuts, running short on continuity, barely
Holding up for the duration. You can see right through me.

When I'm curled up on a vinyl chair, a cheap edition, a Topshop knock-off
With mismatched buckles— when I'm down at hem and misdemeanoured,

Paralysed and uncharismatic, after you've thrown me against a wall
And frisked me— when I'm caught in your ratchets

Inexorable, turning, stretched across a table, stripped
To the core with all my skimpy shanks showing, if then I'm

Off-spindle, missish, lo-fi and hissy,
Tangled, denatured, petty, a crosspatch—

It's because you can expose me.

Telegraphic

The orchids allow for drastic invitation. My last resort

Is cabling you at Spa, where the waters keep their manganese
Secrets below where the fingers of plants taper off

In despair— where you are burrowing behind your silks
And drapery into an elliptical bed, closeted

Among the glass globes' mouths choking with flowers,
Invalid. I have been wasting these two weeks

In an extravagant show of faith, gloved in lavender
And clinging to an ostrich-feather fan, expectant as

The evening primroses in their velvet coats palely
Scattering themselves across the hedge, the bell

On the corner that sounds each hour
When it is not the hour. After you recover

Beneath some canopy of lilies, left over
When the cutting work is through, after

You pick me apart stem by stem in
The porcelain chambers of your head, I will live

On eggshells, chips of bark. You will leave
A new man, not feeling

How I will stick in you: ghost
Limb: wormwood heart.

Monster

I have been away too long. The radios crackle
In continuous forecast: sunken treasure soundings.

Chests of gold are chiselled open. In France, an ancient shark
Sheds its skin of amber. The specimen is well-preserved.

What happens to sleepers when their lids are shut
Is invisible to the world. In a vampire's casket

Lies a lifeless dreamer trying to escape.
I have been singled out by fate

To become a creature that lives in the dark alone. A natural
Craver of attention. A professional moaner.

I am coming back, back
With a trash artist's vengeance, hieratic in eyeliner, marabou

Blonde, back like an automatic
.22 pistol, a sweetheart, a stainless: whiplash

Smart, back in business,
Back with bells on, back spitfire, back sharp.

I have been dangerous,
But now there's no stopping. I have been glamorous,

But not for long enough.
They're calling, they're calling for overtures and beginners—

Flashbulbs everywhere, my dear. Won't you lead me in?

Paris, 1899

Where the trees are thick in their trunks, hard-veined
And pronounced of silhouette. They are disdainers

Knowing how everything fits together, poised among their own
Old world. *I was made for destruction, too improbable*

For this century. When the gas-lights go on they crush together
Awkward and flaring, unschooled in flattery. *They mock me.*

If the day comes I shall stand before you: uncertain
Of voice, unsteady of feature. I shall barely remember

How to signal assent with my hands, much less the words
Orchidaceous and *belated*, least of all

How to account for the distance
From the shimmering, fantastical concoction of my past

To the thing I have become. *Will you find me*
Utterly your own one, still? Along the fraying edges of hems

Our misalliance wanders like pick-stitch, quite crooked
And vanishing when reversed. *We shall not meet again.*

When the day comes I am sure to feel nothing
Even as the continent slowly is shifting, and over

The waters the bells of Trinity and Magdalen are faint in their calls, faintly
Swinging, and when day comes past the houses

In Tite Street the hyacinths will be languid
And astonishing in their finery. *Turn, counterturn, stand.*

Teen Spies

Elijah, Helen, Paul, and me
Clocked the cat by the bikesheds. *1.43.* Kept an eye
Peeled for falsies. Hid in the bushes from Aunt Kay.
Made a dead letter drop and drank Russian tea.

I'm the smallest; Elijah is our control.
Our mission? That's undercover for now. We can't tell
How this enigma will unfold, but we're so full
Of energy we can't come down.

We've got our own lingo and wear special suits—
Study the codebook, radio for supplies,
Draw our cryptic pictures, stay up all night.
We kill time waiting for our lives to start

With log notes: *Saw a demented corgi piss*
On someone's shoe. Shadowed DF back
To his flat. Observed a parrot sat
On someone's head. I am past
                    seventeen and have never been kissed.

Biological

Smallest in the blight, strictest
In the root of a bonfire's glare,
Flawed as an emerald in a Florentine ring. Inextricable

From the narrowest lattice, lacing
The malmaison roses together. We were squandered
By an early dismantlement, the forced

Damage of a transplanted organ in a polythene bag,
Set in a bed of veins with their blue cut ends—
That is, his design was irregular,

Exceeding crabbèd, it was a hood to us
In our close-wrought tower, as we sat together
In a room lined with radiometers, blind and ticking

And when the needle in the spine
Of the rapidograph trembled, it meant
The air was five parts poison on the outer edges, worst

In the burden, the dead bell tolling
When I looked at you, before it was spoilt
And dumb from exposure, after the rope tightened around

The wheel, once it was set in motion we knew
Everything would fall away like a crack
Suddenly opening across the earth, tearing

The corners off the keep. Which was how
We were twice removed from the scene of the crime,
The way the slightest thing becomes visible when fixed

Under water under glass, just that far away
From light.

Blue China

My signs all point to a singular disposition. How shatteringly unpleasant
It is to be born under Sèvres, some doddering holdover
From the *ancien régime*. Weaknesses: vainglory, powder. Those additionally
Half-cusped in Lenox are said to be ill-suited

For industry, desirous of stately homes, and fickle in the extreme. To be
                                                                avoided:
Balconies, timepieces. In the Great Fire
Of 1666, glazing reversed itself and ran down the window-panes
Until every piece of bottle-bottomed glass

Fell out: a dripping Restoration. The curlicues of iron remained
Red-hot and glowing in their frames, a line of crowns
Across the façade of each building. That night clocks rang out in succession
To wake the city where every new chiming-in

Meant another block had gone up, and the spreading pattern of bells
Was a map of the movement of the burning constellation
As it spilled through the streets, westward and processional. It was six
                                                                thousand
Eight hundred and twenty-two o'clock when it ended.

My descent can be traced to a flawed set of plate— Delft in retrograde,
Wedgwood rising— an unfortunate condition. Inclined towards:
Misplacement of items, a high degree of fury. At the collapse of the
                                                        Brighton Pavilion
In 1809, the varnish on the underside of the roof

Gave way first, cracking along fault-lines in a series of thin smiles
Until they covered the ceiling. The painted
Cupids and French roses began missing pieces
At spots that marked where the weakening wood

Was liable to gap. The spars went down like ribbons on their heads,
Feathered and curling into splinters under pressure,
Unseating sixteen dozen white candles from their chandeliers so that
The flames rose up above the ring of columns

To make another roof: a blinding coronation.
My ruling planet is on course for an unsettling destination,
Off-balance and revolving— certain of collision.
The wobble in Dresden predicts a trial by fire.

Every day it gets harder to live up to it.

Love in a Cold Climate I

On the ring road heading south, south of Manchester
Past the crumbling mountains' edges, irregular against the sky, you

Steer, clearing the thin and swooning back-roads, swervers
Through all the hills of these states, where the spindly trees' trunks rise in
masses

From out the cut-granite ground, their leaves
Half alive. There is no landscape where we were driving

In the crumpled corner of the north— only high sides of rock,
A facing of trees, and the small space threading between. In

The convoluted heart of this other England, we were stunning
The way an anomaly of weather patterns snarled over water is stunning,

But lasting no longer than an instant— and this autumn, out on
The motorway you follow the local forecast

Through Worcester and Cambridge, down into Greenwich, on the air-
Waves' heavenly progress to your car.

Love in a Cold Climate II

I was the queen. In a game of charades,
Two fingers mean *concealed*. An avalanche
Was in the wings waiting, the beginners
Frozen on their marks waiting for curtain

Up. My internal anatomy is strange
Like an ice floe on the verge of breaking off
That doesn't, a natural disaster
Like two tonnes of mountain coming down on

A trapped cabin. Let's pretend we're alone
In the empty house: one light left, ghostly,
Still holding on, still huddled, for warmth, then

Pretend that I never pretended to you,
Never kept in the dark a second
Body to warm me— *Finis*. Curtain down.

Divining

On that day, they brought you to the meadow
Where the ground cracked even as you stood

Waiting for the priest to bless you. Their kerchiefs
Were whiter than bones, white for water, not as white

As the stick in your hands. In the quiet
Of their praying you heard the earth, its unforgiving

Snap. Your soles tingled as the splinters widened;
You read the ground and took one step forward.

They thought the rod moved, called by water,
But your hands wrote words as you went across

Your love's body, walking out an apology. You spelled
Your begging with footsteps, holding out

The open hand in your hands, the fork asking
For a few drops, kisses.

France, 1919

Whilst at university, Mao Tse-Tung founded a 'Society for Work and Study in France'. Students of both sexes were sent abroad through this scheme so that they might escape the strictures of traditional Chinese society.

We are the saviours of our country, sipping coffee from cups

From the seventeenth century, three hundred wasted years before
Our revolutionary mouths arrived. Our kiss redeems the invisible
Imprints of a thousand duchesses' lips, our tongues sweet

With justice. At Versailles we take everything
In stride, fifteen black heads occupying mirrors, correcting the clipped
Lines of hedges with our presence. Our hard steps echo off marble, noise

Of how we will make over the world. In Paris we are drunk with revelation
At a city running with modernity— that women can move so long
Of limb, air clean on shaved skin. We will become them.

If we are wide-eyed, we are only new to the world
In which anything is possible, new enough for anyone
To think us immoderate. We want everything

But we cannot take it back. At home
We are only salvagers of the idleness of France,
Broken-hearted and longing for the softest of places, in which everywhere

The unbetrothed hold hands, unknowingly proving us right.

Substitution

First I blindfolded the revolting cat.

I read much lore about chickens: the windowless abbatoir
Found in the French countryside where the slavish Usurper

Laid her ear to the wall, listening to the sound of innumerable chickens
Inside; the coop where reject eggs were thrown and hungry chickens

Came running to eat the yolks. When I held her pet chickens
In my sham embrace, they were unable to detect my subterfuge.

I stole objects from her house one by one, replacing them
With lovingly crafted replicas, until she was living in an imitation

House resembling exactly a real one. In the superfluous space
Of my living-room I built a scale model of her haunts

To acquaint myself with her arena of exploitation.
Also I learned to draw small shrews in 1,126 positions.

At her wedding the fishy minister had proposed, enthralled by
Her white-gloved ability to cause fawning. The best man had already

Succumbed to her auras. I did not want
The slavish bouquet thrown by the Usurper, but it was then

That I conceived my elaborate measures.

I elevated my port to an Usurper-esque height.
It was necessary, moreover, to expand my

Girth. Before, I had been on a private hunger strike
To protest her fleshy bargains. So even her odd rations I readily consumed.

I adopted the Usurper's signature scent, Hypnosis.

I deployed her matt brand of lipstick because her kiss is a veiled
Machination. With mock lashes I enhanced my eyes.

Eventually I could not be distinguished from the Usurper. The way to tell
us apart
Is that she is evil and smiles only at her slaves. Also the way to tell us apart

Is that she is controller of the slaves, which is what I should rightfully be.

Now that the preparations are complete, I do not regret
The rigours entailed by my exquisite method.

I refilled the replacement candy dish with poison

In spherical form. The fabric of the blindfold was spotted black and white,
Like the cat. On it I painted trickily the facsimile eyes.

Defence

When you ask me how I live here, what can I say?
I give you biscuits to feed you, hoping the flour
Will plug your mouth. The crumbs fly out
Like snowflakes. I give you juice to see it come
Dripping from the corners of your mouth. Bits of moisture
Land on your chin.

I twist a dishtowel in my hands, out, in, out
Until it becomes a rope. It burns between my fingers
Like dough. If I dropped it in a tin
And baked it, by the time it was done
My hands would be so raw I couldn't touch the platter.
You'd slice it up, swallow bites between sentences.

I watch my palms when you talk. The mounds of flesh
Look hard, like wood. Clouds of blood
And fortune lines seem to ridge, then darken. I watch your lips,
Which crease and pull the consonants. The recess of your chin
Is where you keep the vowels dry. The points of your collar
Rest under your throat. When you ask me how I live,
I look at my hands. These are my weapons.

Portrait at Windsor

FIRE BREAKS OUT INSIDE WINDSOR CASTLE;
SEVERAL PAINTINGS DESTROYED
The New York Times, *November 1992*

This great heat sets my face to cracking.
A web of wrinkles creeps across me, my skin
Is peeling. Each flake is crisp and falling.

They cannot stop my slow dismantling; it is a dry
Season. The smoke undoes me, it eats
Around my edges. Each brushstroke crumbles.

I came here in a Gothic season: new-gilt,
True-grained, cut from the very heart
Of the trunk. I came dressed

In velvet, lush, glistening
With varnish, precious as nothing else
Ever was. For four hundred and sixty-one years

I have been a queen. I shall go out
In this uneven light, fading
By the flaring light of the heart of one

November, beating
Out the hours of the afternoon of a year gone to ash.
For four hundred and sixty-one years, I kept

This place. There will not be another.

Seaside Resorts

In Blackpool, I fainted dead on the spot.
The Illuminations were a gleam in the head donkey's eye,
Which eyed us suspiciously.

At Margate your ice-cream fell off its cone.
We settled for green-apple rock instead.

Between us something like Sussex lies— crab-shaped,
Humped in the middle, not quite symmetrical.
On the underside, tiny coves like mouths.

Boats landed at Hastings like bats coming home.
Their noses questioned me pointedly.

Combined, we would make an acceptable picnic spot,
Patchy in places. Birds on a branch, each a small container,
Containing bird-organs. And flocked.

On the end of Bournemouth pier, my boater flew into the Channel.
Luckily the candyfloss clung fast to its stick.

We are skirting England along its fringes, widdershins,
Like witches. A necklace circling a strange neck.
We outline the shape of it.

Torquay. The pebbles chattered under your feet.

Parliament of Fowls

Wherever we shiver,
With our alliance of knifing, the air, it turns

Cataclysmic over Westminster, wheeling through the acid-holed
Barcelonan lacework, past the yellow knobs of Chartres

And licks the steps up the Grotekirk's spire. This is the blood sport
We aim at through the keyhole of the clay trap's

Eye, the cross-stitched leather snares of the beaters hiding
In raked haystacks with pocketfuls of lead.

Our shadow cabinet speeds over continents, missile
And arrives in one blow— a dark hood over the head of the heath,

Feet hooked round the spun-metal cord
That electrifies the shires. Backbenchers take to their nooks

Between the sharp-edged slats that fence
Our chamber. We have lingered

Amongst your cabbage roses, fondled the grain
Of your fur-lined gloves— now our Chancellor of the Quiver

Declares it open season. Your century is over.

House

The bat that scrabbled in the wall of the kitchen, all winter
The electric nerves running down to the scanty socket
The drills boring holes in the concrete foundation
And the fumes just keep rising from the mysterious oven

When the wolf's at the door and the door isn't locking
When the penny drops and you're stood there, staring
What happens after the feet start moving
The next thing you know is the sound of running

The clockwork bent back in a crooked frame
The blackout blinds down and the ceiling fan
Then: one little pig in the open air, a trotter

Just lifted, snuffling this way and that, putting
Its nose to the ground, down to the business of surviving
On trash or anything that keeps its dumb brain going

Fête Champêtre

In Watteau the women are faceless and turning
Their backs on us, gracefully, swaddled in frocks
Pale pink, hyacinth, old gold, flickering
Silver in the creases of their vanishing

Limbs. They permit only a delicate touch
As if fading, already, from human sight
Into the darkening woods, receding
Like ghosts into shapelessness, into thin air.

Off to the side, a man leans towards the dim
Corner where first two narrow legs emerge,
Then the red and blue diamonds across the suit,

Neck-ruffled, skull-capped. It is the Harlequin
Looking us in the eye, unmasked and still
Expressionless, as if no-one were near.

Vesuvius (In the Priests' Quarters)

When it came, we were getting ready
For bed. The gowns lay on the mattresses,
White as palms open for a coin.

I always loved how they spread themselves,
Armless and headless, across the sheets,
Loved that perfect stillness of things

Dropped from a great height. They stretched
The length of the beds like so many
Paper dolls. That night

The sandals waited on the floor, soft
Brown mouths, open and dumb as those
Of oxen. I loved how the feet

Came down with a slap, the straps
An embrace. We were kneeling
When it hit. Through the window

I saw its hand and when the others ran
I stood, walked the row
Putting on each pair of sandals, pulling

One crackling cloth over my head after another.

III

Shoemaker's Holiday

All they that love not Tobacco and Boies are fools.

Richard Baines, 1593

Heel-block and stopper, cone of thread, dresser,
The four awls and stirrups, hand and thumb
　Leathers: 'St Hugh's bones' lie spread out before me.
If I am part æther, un-earthly
　Of humour, it could be surmised
My mother was a sempster. Theirs is a guild notorious
　For patience. Yet I am more probable
To yield to temptation. I've a weakness for
　Tea-drinking, for tobacco and boys, for any
Riot of horn-blowers that comes down the street.
　Rubbing-pin, paring knife, bucket
Of nails: if I am, on occasion, a touch
　Temperamental, it might be because I was kitted-out
For frivolity. Flashing of needles and flicker of satin,
　Ribbon-curler, shirrer, an excess of beading—
Notorious angel, I am apprentice to no-one.
　I think a little playing up would be forgiven.

Revenger's Tragedy

You don't return my calls. In a month of missing days
Everything thwarts me, even the curls of my hair freeze;

My skin sheds, leaving flakes on my wool sweater. We are erratic
Both, changing with the weather, but you think of it

As an astronomical progression. Last year you called me
Your little sunflower. Eleven blizzards later I think of how

To get you: calculating mercury, sighting along constellations,
Rehearsing the lines of a paid assassin— *not know me, my Lord?*

You cannot choose! I bide time,
Hoarse-tongued and blue as poison, the double

Line of my eyes gone to slits. I hate like a tooth hurts,
At the root. I will startle the bones

From their sockets, they will crack like glass
And catch in your throat. I will dazzle

Your heart from its cage. The lungs will knock and clap
Together in the empty place. The applause will make you rattle.

Rhode Island Waltz

We tilt five degrees
Off of true, precarious in photograph, stiff

In three-quarter time. Our rotation
Is unnatural as architecture. A palace seen in cross-section,

Fiercely rendered. A mansard roof slipping
From the lintels in stop-motion, intricate

In betrayal. This is me before the car starts moving
In the space beside you, in a debutante hour, when the lights

On houses are just starting to glow: thin-fingered
And dangerously fine of wrist, sketching

The ruins of a building twisted in the middle
Whose walls are surprised to find themselves

Skewed. That was me on the corner
Of Angell Street, where a line of sparrows suddenly halted, below

A branch cut clean through, before a window
Gone off-kilter, me on tiptoe

Trying not to touch you where you stopped
In the bare centre of a world, perfect in scale

To ascertain the angle of each elevation,
Learning the sight-lines off by heart.

Alchemy

If it could be done, I'd do it
In an instant. I've got the charts,
The mortar and pestle, the fullest
Array of flasks this side of Rome.
My walls are papered with symbols, and the biggest
Is gold. There's a cabinet full
Of rejects: salt and cow hair,
Rye harvested under a full moon and tin,
Magnesium and saints' spit. I could show you
Calculation, the reams of vellum in my closet, enough
Ink for ten octopi. Instead I promise you piles of gold,
Shining heaps higher than
Your bed, weighing more
Than the both of us.

At night I sit alone, poring
Over books in older tongues; none
Of the words are in my dictionary.
Signs stare down at me— calcium, Saturn,
Silver, lead— mean as Chinese, like a maze.
When I fall asleep I dream the metals
And planets sweep me up, wrap me
In their dark mesh bed and I can't see
To read any more. But I wake to
The jars of cow parts, the cup and balance
Waiting to measure, and the open mouths of flasks
That say *You will still be hungry*
When you are full.

Exercises

Readying for bed, I take the now-familiar stance,
Back against the wall, arms bent,
Locked in a figure like an anatomical model.
Press and release is how I keep count.

To learn to use an artificial limb
The body must become artificial itself,
Learn how to move, then move like a machine.
Tendon, tunnel, muscle, sheath.

It seems I cannot change myself enough.
After my tooth was extracted, they planted
A screw and a screw in the gap, then added
A fake tooth on top, but it didn't take.

I don't believe things happen for a reason.
I don't remember what it was like before.
Press, release, repeat, repeat.
I can't tell whether it makes me stronger.

Self-Portrait After Vermeer

Already I am too old, coming to
An appointment 7,417 days late, penitent

In pearls and homespun, high-waisted, tied up
With muslin: an Old Master. I've got to break

For it and believe
There is another way, that curtains can be drawn

Over windows, voracious
Dreams; somehow

To count slow enough
Under my breath to go

Unseen. I am crouching behind you,
Trying to shrink and failing

Fast. But in this kind of divine
Light I am transfigurable, re-

Formed, chimærical. There are those who doubt
And those who wait. I will keep coming

Late, playing my age, framing myself
While you steal a little here and now.

NOTES

Double Wedding, 1615: 'No other jewels hang about our necks than these' is adapted from a line from *Edward II*, by Christopher Marlowe.

The Pre-Raphælites: 'What *do* you mean by beauty?' is quoted from the song 'Orchid Girl', by Aztec Camera.

Monster: This poem bears no relation to the film of the same title.

Paris, 1899: 'I was made for destruction' is quoted from a letter by Oscar Wilde.

Blue China: The Brighton Pavilion doesn't feature a ring of columns and has never collapsed.

Love in a Cold Climate I: The New England region of America contains hundreds of places named after English ones, including the towns of Manchester, Worcester, Cambridge, and Greenwich.

Shoemaker's Holiday: The shoemaking tools in the first three lines are mentioned (in a different order) in *The Shoemaker's Holiday*, by Thomas Dekker. 'St Hugh's bones' was a colloquial expression for such tools, he being the patron saint of shoemakers. 'Sempster' is the period form of the word 'seamstress'.

Revenger's Tragedy: 'Not know me, my Lord? You cannot choose!' is quoted from *The Revenger's Tragedy*, by Thomas Middleton.